You Can Live Cheaply Too

During and After COVID-19

Camille Rogers-Jones

Copyright © 2020 Camille Rogers-Jones and You Can Too Motivation

All Rights Reserved. No part of this publication may be reproduced in any form or by any means, including scanning, photocopying, or otherwise without prior written permission of the copyright holder.

Disclaimer and Terms of Use: The Author and Publisher have strived to be as accurate and complete as possible in the creation of this book, notwithstanding the fact they do not warrant or represent at any time that the contents within are accurate. While all attempts have been made to verify information provided in this publication, the Author and Publisher assume no responsibility for errors, omissions, or contrary interpretation of the subject matter herein. Any perceived slights of specific persons, peoples, or organizations are unintentional. In practical advice books, like anything else in life, there are no guarantees of personal results. This book is not intended for use as a source of legal, business, accounting, medical, or financial advice. All readers are advised to seek services of competent professionals in the legal, business, accounting, medical, and finance fields.

Dedicated to the world's essential workers during COVID-19.

Table of Contents

Introduction: Living Cheaply During and After COVID-19 – Applying Scenario Planning..... 1

Chapter 1: Focal Issues - Identifying Why You Want or Need to Live Cheaply........................ 7

Chapter 2: Cheaper Monthly Bills................ 15

Chapter 3: Cheap Family Entertainment and Gifts 27

Chapter 4: Cheap Shopping Tips.................. 37

Chapter 5: Cheap Easy Meals to Make 47

Chapter 6: Clothing Cheaply and Stylishly After COVID-19.. 59

Chapter 7: Cheaper Travel – Scenario Planning for the Unknown............................ 67

Chapter 8: Cheap Living Constantly During and After COVID 85

Appendices 91

About the Author... 95

Introduction: Living Cheaply During and After COVID-19 – Applying Scenario Planning

The cost of living throughout the world is more expensive than ever. COVID-19 has changed the world we once knew, and in some areas prices for essential items are doubling with some supplies running out. All too often we find ourselves spending our hard-earned cash on day to day living with nothing left for fun as the lockdown restrictions are slowly relaxed. Moving forward things like fun, entertainment, and travel will eventually return but with likely price fluctuations. Living cheaply will need to be a necessity until worldwide economies grow again and local spending begins to increase as we venture out of our homes. This we can accomplish by borrowing clever *business scenario planning* strategies and employing helpful money-saving tips.

Cheap living is easy – when you know how. The reality is many of us have been doing it since COVID first swept across the globe.

What I will share with you in this book is not rocket science; it's from personal time-tested experiences and techniques now applied to living during and after COVID-19. I will share with you how we lived before, and especially our tips on how to accomplish it more cheaply. We have applied these even more strictly during COVID times and have managed to save even more than in times prior. Living cheaply during COVID-19 has become a necessary way of life for many people and families throughout the entire world.

The key in the future will be to save for a rainy day, a non-essential dream, or, God forbid, another pandemic. We still need our dreams and hopes, and plan to safely enjoy them. *Scenario planning* (in business terms) means planning for uncertainty – and that is certainly the times we are living in, now and looking ahead. I have borrowed greatly from this business process in anticipation of possible economically undesirable outcomes during and after COVID-19. Accordingly, aspects of scenario planning like external forces (COVID-19) and *critical uncertainties* (budget and finances) underpin our home lives and financial futures. Subsequently, the process of scenario planning, tips, and strategies in this book can greatly help with achieving a valuable habit of living cheaply even as we recover from this crisis.

I believe as we move forward it will be not only important, but an essential responsibility, to reduce, reuse, and recycle (not just save money) to ensure that the healing the planet began during the shutdowns is maintained. Throughout our experiences as foster-parents, and also providing care for over 25 children, my husband and I have willingly embraced this lifestyle in order to reduce our carbon footprint and ensure the children who have lived with us (and more who are to come!) have an enriched life. I think these experiences prepared us well for COVID times. The kids who have lived with us have, even during lockdown, respected life needs as becoming a bit different for a little while. Our household bills have been significantly reduced, and with the savings we have made we've been able to provide them with the best education and medical needs, and can even plan ahead in anticipation of some luxurious holidays! Living cheaply has become an essential lifestyle change and choice for those who want to save money and be respectful to the planet. Regardless of your circumstances, living cheaply means you and your family will eat well, live well, and eventually travel well, not to mention study well and retire well more cheaply. How nice it will be when the 'pause' button becomes 'play' again as the world transforms into a COVID-safe environment.

Your new "living cheaply lifestyle change" may have stemmed from COVID-19, a job loss, reduced income, saving for retirement, or saving for a holiday or college fund. My household is living proof that if you live cheaply day to day during and after COVID times, you and your family will be the richer for it. And we don't just mean financially.

Prior to COVID, our first step was simply knowing we had to make a change to a cheaper lifestyle. It's your first step, too, if you haven't taken it yet. Maybe you are lucky like me and have been able to work from home, or, sadly, like one of my friends you have gone from a six-figure job to being stood down. Another friend got a new job during the middle of COVID on higher pay, with less responsibility, fewer hours, and the opportunity to work from home. Regardless, learning how to continue to live cheaply is an important skill. By now, because of circumstances, you have most likely identified how and what to change. If you haven't, at first this may seem overwhelming – but don't worry. I will share with you our useful resources that provide helpful tips and

Introduction: Applying Scenario Planning

suggestions which, along with scenario planning skills, will enable you to plan for a variety of circumstances and help you forge the road ahead.

Your enforced COVID-19 lifestyle change begins with changing your mindset (and family's mindset) to a sustainable affordable lifestyle including ways to shop differently, create cheap meals that the whole family will enjoy, find affordable clothing, provide cheap family fun, locate entertainment and cheap travel, save money on your monthly expenses and utilities, and most importantly learn how to keep living cheaply once you have made the "cheap lifestyle change." In summary, this book aims to encourage you to utilize the scenario planning skills of "what if" and start making reasonable assumptions about how the COVID-19 future looks. It involves identifying realities and uncertainties to improve financial outcomes. For you this means transforming the home setting as you identify, change, plan, anticipate, and alter your lifestyle as required. We did it. You can, too.

You Can Live Cheaply Too During and After COVID-19

Chapter 1: Focal Issues - Identifying Why You Want or Need to Live Cheaply

The first step to living more cheaply utilizing *scenario planning* is the process of identifying the *focal issue*. It is strategic and essential to identify exactly why you are changing your lifestyle. What will you focus upon? What can you change? People opt to change their lifestyle for many different reasons. Which is yours? Applying scenario planning skills to your home front is a great strategy to help prioritize and plan for different situations impacted by the fallout of COVID-19 and help you save dollars.

1. Sustainability

Over-consumerism and wastage are two common reasons why our natural resources are being depleted and the ecological balance of our world is turning upside down. The four prongs of sustainability, economical, environmental, and social focuses should encourage anyone (regardless of their personal circumstances) to reduce, reuse, recycle, and, as I discuss in the next few chapters, re-purpose. By this I mean to re-purpose everything including your spending/shopping habits, cooking habits (and what you do with the leftovers), clothing habits, entertainment habits, utility usage, and future travel plans. In doing so you will be making your day to day life affordable, and you will **enable our planet to have a future**.

2. COVID-19 Has Caused Even More Families to Have Reduced Incomes

Living cheaply and sustainably for low income families is now considered "the new normal" thanks to COVID-19, and has become a necessity for nearly everyone. Lower income earners, with clever money management, can create many opportunities otherwise not affordable. You can live "even cheaper than cheap." You can supplement your income with home-based work strategies which I will unpack later in this book. By shifting your mindset to a positive "I can do this" mode you will **enable yourself to be resourceful and develop momentum to improve your circumstances.**

3. COVID-19 Employment Change or Retrenchment

We all live in a COVID-19 world where a virus and technology has drastically changed the nature of employment. A person experiencing retrenchment may be quickly forced to make cutbacks. Perhaps you have had a change of jobs and now work your "dream job" that does not pay as much? Since the GFC and COVID-19 many doors have closed, leaving not just individuals but whole towns without a job or traditional income. New enterprises (especially working from home) are taking over from the previous drudgery of a 9-5 workday. Maybe you wanted to work from home to care for and enjoy precious moments with your children while they were young? No problem during COVID-19 – but how will you manage that arrangement moving forward? Are you a guardian like me, who will need to continue to work from home? Regardless of the circumstances, the following chapters will help you greatly. Identifying the reasons why you want to live cheaply ***enables you to scenario plan effectively in order to anticipate inevitable unknowns such as retrenchment, and thus make maintainable decisions.***

4. Reducing Accrued Debt

Debt, whether it is a "good debt" like a college loan, home loan, or investment property loan, or a "bad debt" like a maxed-out credit card (guilty as charged in my non-frugal previous life!), *a debt is a debt*. If you can't get debt under control, it's stressful having it hang over your head. It's difficult to resist accepting another debt to pay off the old debt, which may be an attractive temporary solution because of COVID-19 times. Of course if it's your only option you may need to take it. However, you will need to change your original overspending and "living beyond your means" habits. The truth is that creating a new debt is not going to change those looming realities. You will only end up accruing more debt upon old debt. Then it becomes a vicious cycle to break. It might help to re-consolidate your debt, but that solution will only work if you pay it down quickly and change your spending habits, replacing them with good ones. Reducing overhead by living a cheaper lifestyle ***enables you to pay down your outstanding debt more quickly to put yourself and your family in a better financial situation.***

5. Creating a Luxury Retirement

Your 401k, Superannuation, or government-based pension scheme may not be enough to make retirement comfortable. It certainly won't allow you to retire early, especially now if it has dipped during COVID-19. From an early earning age this knowledge should be kept as a priority. Perhaps you have been lucky enough, and/or worked hard enough, to have a lucrative wage every week. Then one day you suddenly retire, and the only way your retirement savings will last is by living a cheaper lifestyle. Perhaps you plan on living off your retirement savings and have a part time job. Has COVID-19 affected your investments so that you are now forced to find employment years after finishing work?

Maybe you want to finally start creating the opportunity to add more money to your retirement fund, or perhaps you need to even start one. Will you have enough? How do you make more? Has COVID-19 affected your nest egg or earning capacity? Better to **enable yourself now to live cheaply and create a wealthier retirement future, while you still can.**

Utilizing Key Scenario Planning Skills:

Our own scenario planning tool kit includes these actionable affirmations:

1. Decide/anticipate/forecast why you are going to living more cheaply. Our reasons were "all of the above!" Remember that living cheaply does not mean living poorly. End of discussion.

2. We wanted to be innovative and improve our *adaptability* skills, so we always remembered the fact children follow our lead, and so do yours. We quickly realized how to "sell" these changes positively. Avoid negative statements like, "We have to save money." Instead, phrase it more positively such as, "Wow, we can use the money we save for..." Language is powerful. We have been careful to say positive statements during the current health crisis like, "COVID-19 will eventually end, let's look forward to what we can do after," and, "This is just a pause, not stop."

3. Budgeting for the unexpected, so any monies (even small) left over after all the necessities were paid for was a HUGE motivator. Do not underestimate this! Continue to make plans for small luxuries, travel, college funds, and retirement. Involve the whole family when making those kinds of decisions. Ownership is empowering; projecting what you want your future to look like and how to get there is paramount.

4. *Embracing change* was something that happened very quickly during COVID. Decline in consumerism during COVID is actually an asset if you allow yourself to really see it. We often have already been "consumerised." I advise you to "de-consumerise" yourself and your family. It will not be as difficult as you think. COVID times are prodding us in that direction, and the truth is almost everyone cares about the environment. Reducing wastage, re-using, re-cycling, and re-purposing are thus important life skills; living cheaply teaches this by example. It's not only about saving money; it's about also helping the planet.

5. Clear *Communication* is essential, just as in my family we wanted to improve our communication with each other we found our fun and enjoyment as a family actually increased from living cheaply. That makes living cheaply priceless.

Chapter 2: Cheaper Monthly Bills

Scenario planning often involves determining a list of key factors from the focal issue (living cheaply) – in reducing overhead. As part of our key factor list, forecasting how much we could easily save in our budget by living cheaply was our priority as we focused on how to reduce our bills and expenses. We identified that the most expensive items were utility bills, shopping, meals, entertainment, and clothing. Whether you are single, live with flatmates, or have a family, all of these savings add up very quickly to help you save big dollars.

Let's start with utility bills. Not all of us are lucky enough to have access to solar power or other expensive new technologies. If you have not already investigated this category of savings during lockdown, do so now! Electricity and utilities add a hefty dent into your monthly bills. What if I told you that there are ways to save on your current bills? What if I told you that you could make money by helping others do the same? What if I told you that you could work from home? What if I told you that you could earn good commissions while helping other people save money? What if I told you that you could make passive, residual money every month? I'm going to share with you some secrets not many people know about and some success stories of people I know personally who have turned their lives around – all while saving hundreds and thousands every year on utility bills.

What if I also told you that you can save even more money on your phone, home internet, insurance, and also help others while making passive residual income? Not only am I going to tell you how, I'm also going to share the direct contact details of a group who can help you. Not interested in earning passive income? No problem, I'm still going to give you some great ideas on how to save money with your bills so that by the end of the month you will have made significant savings.

Save Energy for Future Generations

The biggest hurdle with teenagers was constantly reminding them to turn lights and electronic devices off. From the kettle, toaster, television, ceiling fan, air-conditioner, computer charger, and phone charger, some of them have been so wasteful. I have a speech I give every time they leave one on. They now know that if they are caught they get "the speech." They do not like the speech. It is repeated verbatim in a sarcastic tone. They now turn things off. If they do occasionally forget, not only do they get the speech, they get less screen time. There is a nice lesson in there for them. If they are respectful, instead of wasteful, they earn the right to use it. Pretty simple.

As a parental figure to many teenage girls, I breathe a sigh of relief that curly, natural hair styles are coming back. Two big ticket electricity suckers are actually hair straighteners and hair dryers. Our girls know those items only come out for special occasions, not for a school day. Yes, you hear them gasp – I know. But there's a trick I use. The girls do their hair on a Friday morning with all the gadgets. That way they get Friday day, the weekend, and even Monday with their idea of "perfect hair." The other days have become up-style and braiding days. Not surprisingly, they get many compliments about their hair on the weekdays because up-styles, braiding, and the trusty ponytail are stylish.

The other biggest energy users in the household are your refrigerator, dishwasher, clothes washer and dryer. An energy efficient appliance really helps here. Always spread your cold goods around in the fridge in their specific compartments. This also helps reduce wastage of your food by categorizing it in the fridge. As simple as it may sound, place your cheeses together, your fruits and vegetables in their drawers, etc. That way everyone knows where everything is all the time. Parents worldwide have wondered (no doubt like me!) "how long can you actually stare into a refrigerator with the door open?" Checking on the cooling elements of your refrigerator and cleaning your fridge regularly also helps reduce energy usage and create savings (especially check for dust).

Cut Costs During and After COVID with Timers and Off-Peak Usage

Just by changing to energy efficient, low peak periods you can quickly cut your heating and cooling expenses by as much as $200-$800. Whether you live on your own or with a tribe-load of kids who constantly need to turn a heater on instead of putting on a cardigan, setting specific times for your heating and cooling will dramatically help you save money and energy. When appliance shopping, always try and purchase one with a good energy rating. This means you have control over reducing energy output.

When it comes to monthly heating and cooling costs, use a programmable timer that adjusts for the less expensive usage times. For example, set your hot water system to heat up overnight, not during the daytime. This alone can save hundreds of dollars.

Invest in Renewable Energy with a "Light Bulb Moment"

We recently moved to a house with solar power. I cannot believe the difference in our bill. There are many companies who offer upfront panels and installation with government backed discounts and payment plans. The savings here are significant over the life of the panels. We saved further money by installing a gas hot water system. I'd estimate a savings of over $600 a year. By going solar and switching electricity providers (see below) our average bill for a family of four has more than halved.

Whether it's LEDs or CFL lights, converting all of your light bulbs in your household to Energy Star compact fluorescent light bulbs or light-emitting diodes will save big dollars over long periods as they use 3/4 less energy than other bulbs. I used to dread getting on a chair and trying to unscrew a light bulb. Now, we rarely need to change them. The other great thing about using LEDs or CFLs is they generate less heat than standard bulbs. We stock up when they are on sale, and because they last longer we get almost ten times more usage than a standard bulb. The kids know never to leave a light on. They also know not to leave any appliance like TV, kettle, or toaster on standby.

Water Wise for the Planet, Not Just Bills and Saving Tips

If you don't already know to turn off the bathroom tap while you are brushing your teeth or washing your hands, you do now! Constantly running faucets uses up a lot of water. We switched to water saving taps and showerheads a long time ago. Not only is this going to be a huge savings in the long run, but your bathroom and kitchen will get a makeover! We took a little from our savings from budgeting and paid for a plumber to check for leaks and drips. Often, people don't want to fork over for the plumber to do a "plumbing health check," but this is shortsighted and doing so is a smart way to save money in the long run. Our plumbers installed water saving heads which included a warranty for both product and installation.

We only wash our clothes and household items during non-peak electricity time, and only use the dryer when necessary, such as a bout of bad weather or if there are no more clean uniforms or school clothes to wear. Try hanging wet washing on hangers in winter inside, where you may be using indoor heat already or have a fireplace going. Look at the weather forecast for the week ahead. Time the washing for a predicted sunny day. Limit your washing loads each week. We have one day a week where we wash our clothes and household linens. (I said we. We all take it turns to do the washing.)

Each week there is a load of household whites and colors. Some weeks we may have more than one load of each, of course, but we have trained the kids to soak their whites in the soaking tub the day before washing day, as do we. This keeps them fresh and white. We only use the eco cycle on the washer. We have a 15 minute wash cycle. I love it: NO wasted water, and washing is quicker and less laborious. A big hint here is to wash only in cold water with a good powder. Our electricity is off-peak so our hot water system heats up at night. Washing in cold water means less electricity is needed.

We have gas hot water and adjustable thermostats. Adjusting the temperature of your water heater will reduce your heating and water bills! Alter the use of your garden sprinklers to off-peak time. Try to only run your sprinklers once or twice a week instead of daily. And did you know you can purchase energy saving sprinklers? Check with your local government, too, to see if you can divert your washing water to your gardens for irrigation.

Showering and bathing during non-peak time also saves considerable money. We have a rule in our house. Where we live is currently drought declared, so we are all very aware of water conservation. We have reduced the use of the bathtub to one bath per week for the young kids, and instead substitute quick showers. This significantly reduces usage. Kids waste time and water when taking a bath. Bathing has become play time, not essential cleaning yourself time. It's a bit like when I see parents in public who for most of their child's life have shoved a tablet or phone into their hand to keep them entertained, especially while at a restaurant or café. Then they wonder why their teenagers expect the gadgets to still be at the table? So, bath time is out, and quick showering is in.

When showering, each person is allowed only one short song's worth of hot water per day. This is more than enough time to do the daily essentials. We encourage them to choose a 2-3 minute song, with the exception of "washing your hair day" or "shaving your legs day" for the female teens. In order to have a longer shower, they have to have quicker showers during the rest of the week. Me, I have learned to be really, really, quick on most days in order to accrue my long shower time. I listen to *Purple Rain* by Prince or *November Rain* by Guns and Roses. But, even on my long shower day I never get to the end of either song. The best thing apart from conserving water and saving money from the hot water bill is that there is no longer a traffic jam in the bathroom!

Passive Income Through Essential Bills

I want to make you aware of energy wholesalers. These are businesses who specialize in securing huge discounts on your utility bills. The best thing about them is if you also want to help your family members and friends save money on their bills, you can sign up and become a wholesaler and pass on great savings while earning a commission for yourself. To save money on your bills you simply sign up, and the wholesaler will then identify how to save money on your bills and expenses by finding the best company for your needs.

In our case, we have saved approximately 35% through our consultants at *Happy Times Essential Services Consultancy*. We have saved a staggering amount with this company. Its owners Mari and Jason Yaxley are passionate about helping people and improving the quality of life for their customers, as well as helping charities. You can find them at:

www.HappyTimes.acnibo.com

Mari and Jason are based in Australia, but have access to worldwide deals wherever you may live. This is a worldwide business.

Apart from helping you achieve cheaper essential bills, if you'd like to become a wholesaler yourself and earn passive income from commissions, they can guide you and mentor you through that process. The easy learning and setup all occurs online. As dedicated consultants, they help you save money on essential bills like utility, internet, phone, insurance, EFTPOS, security and automation, and gas. They can find these huge discounts for you as they are partnered with their parent company who has mass buying power, enabling them to deal directly with providers and pass on wholesale prices to you. They help you turn bills into passive income, and in most cases end up making your own electricity bill free! With funding from their business Happy Times Essential Services Consultancy, they have purchased land in Brazil with the view to establish a center for homeless children and victims of domestic violence while also providing funds to numerous charities. They talk to each individual customer and manage everything for them while also offering the opportunity to join their team and work from home to make passive income. Please contact them directly using the link above.

You can research online about energy wholesaler consultants and companies. Most "mom and pop" wholesalers work from home making regular passive income commissions while saving family, friends, and clients huge amounts on their bills. Who does not like cheaper bills or the prospect to earn money in the process?

You Can Live Cheaply Too During and After COVID-19

Chapter 3: Cheap Family Entertainment and Gifts

There is no point in improving your personal cash flow unless you intend to enjoy your life with your new savings. Scenario planning involves anticipating different possible narratives. One of those narratives is, most importantly, how does family life improve with alternative forms of free or cheap entertainment and gifts? Creating your own family narrative of enjoyable lifelong memories is ultimately why we all go to work in the first place. So, learning how to have fun cheaply will immensely help your family to remember COVID times as surprisingly manageable and happy. While it may seem a lifetime ago with the pandemic (and I'm certain that when cinemas open again it will be something we all long for as a treat every now and then again) movies at the cinema and all the trimmings that go with it (such as popcorn, drinks, and candy) is not a cheap night out, and never has been! Sporting events are also a money sucker, but are a favorite past time for many, especially in our family. Living cheaply doesn't mean you have to miss out on these things. By now, you have started to calculate your savings accruing from small changes you have made during COVID-19. You most likely have enough to afford small luxuries with your savings already. However, some of your best COVID times have been at home or in your neighborhood. Don't lose sight of that!

Before and during COVID times, in our house we have alternated between different types of activities we do together. We often treat the kids to their own favorite thing as part of their birthday or Xmas presents. We are big believers in "presence" not just presents for family fun and activities. Below are our favorites. I hope you enjoy them, too. Family fun, enjoyment, and laughter don't have to be expensive. I will share with you techniques for finding cheaper tickets to various places for family outings after COVID-19, too!

Leaderboard Family Board Game Nights

Do not underestimate the competitive nature humans possess. Whenever I see board games at the secondhand store or in department stores, I snap them up. Some of our best family time has been with the humble board game or playing charades. Before COVID-19, even the kids' friends liked coming for a sleepover on game night. We have ongoing competitions and even score keeping for Monopoly, Scrabble, Checkers, Chess, Charades, and the family favorite Celebrity Heads (guessing the celebrity name on your forehead). We aim to have one afternoon or night a week for family fun, and will interchange movie night with board game night, an outdoor activity, or even a camping trip away (last weekend it was in the backyard!) where we play games. You have probably rediscovered this yourself during the health crisis. Keep doing it when it is over. No doubt it has been fun! Of course, we keep a leaderboard with some fun rewards for the winners.

Who's the Best Chef?

Another great family activity that you can do for free is having a family cooking night – think *Master Chef*, *Iron Chef*, *My Kitchen Rules*, etc. Kids love cooking and baking things, and they will love the idea of getting to bake something themselves. Flatmates can have a cook-off challenge. For the kids (and big kids too!) try baking cookies or small cakes and then decorating them with creative and beautiful toppings. So, the next time you are planning your family fun night or flatmate night in, try incorporating the meal prep and cooking for a bit of added fun. It will save you money and still give you and your family lots of fun and excitement! If you are part of an urban family, and especially if you are single, these kinds of family activities are just as important and you will relish the memories someday.

Virtual Fun and Challenges

There are many free apps, games, videos, brainteasers, and even free movies nowadays. And all are available online in the comfort of your home in your pajamas! Now more than ever our world is turning to the internet for virtually (pun intended) everything, and you and your frugal family can also. The best part is it is instantaneous, fun, and often free. I won't list those sites; by now you have found them and your kids are likely already kept entertained by them while at home. There are also sites you can go to create games. Now that is cool!

Family or Flatmate Movie Night

This is a favorite in our house. We each have a turn in choosing the movie to watch together, with the preference being a comedy. We recently took our shopping savings and signed up to Netflix. I also found a handy item online during a sale: a $25 "throw projector." The way this works is we log onto the computer and "throw the movie" on the white wall in the house. If you don't have a white wall, you can often find and use a cheap white window blind. My friend found one at the second-hand store, cleaned it up some, and now has created her own handy "drop down cinema screen."

Before we watch the movie, we make homemade pizza from left over sandwich meats like salami or ham on generic frozen pizza or pizza crusts that are on sale. We are very Italian in our approach, using minimal toppings with lots of flavor. Kids love making pizza. I always have at the ready tomatoes and basil leaves (from the garden of course) for toppings. They surprisingly love this, and of course ham and cheese, the most. Sometimes we time the movie night when the local pizza store does their $5 pizza night. I also have in the cupboard red and white stripe popcorn cartons for our delicious home-made popcorn, and brown paper bags for the candy buffet I place out. I often find (at discount stores and the local supermarket) cheap confectionaries and candy.

For less than $10 a week, including the Netflix subscription and food, movie night in our house is fabulous! I can tell you that during

COVID this sense of "normalcy" has worked wonders on our morale.

We will still go to the cinema for a fraction of the normal cost after COVID, as we pre-buy our tickets or find deals online where the tickets are as little as $5-$10 per ticket. We have purchased from Groupon, RACQ, and various other discounted ticket sites. For birthdays we try to always give the kids prepaid movie tickets. We always explain to them to take their movie snacks from home. Of course, some of our stubborn kids/teenagers didn't like doing that, but they soon realized that for the same cost of popcorn and a drink at the cinema they could see another two movies – so, they soon got over it! We look forward to going to the cinema again one day soon. (I may or may not be dreaming of seeing Chris Hemsworth or Dwayne Johnson at a cinema near us soon.)

Choose your Own Camping and Fitness Adventure

You can keep camping simple and invest in a sturdy tent and sleeping bags. It's so handy to have a holiday on a budget and be out with nature. When things open-up again it is not only one of the first things we want to do, it's the first holiday opportunity that will open up. If you need any equipment, many online stores are having huge sales. Also, second-hand stores usually have camping equipment. The best thing is you can always find the spare parts missing from tents at the same second-hand store you bought it from!

If you have the tent and build up your camping equipment cheaply and gradually (easily done online) then there will be many inexpensive trips and holidays always at the ready. You can even be super-organized like us and get some *glamping* under your belt. There are so many camping and RV grounds which are inexpensive and have extra amenities like water slides, pools, outdoor movie screens, etc. for the fraction of the cost of a hotel. We, like many others, have been camping in our backyard during COVID. This has proven that even the backyard can provide family camping fun, as kids have a great imagination. Remember: where there is a campfire, toast the generic marshmallows!

Where we live in Queensland, there are both coastal and hinterland trails and walks. This inexpensive activity can become addictive, and has helped us greatly in our exercising during COVID-19. We sometimes give the kids an Instagram challenge to see who can take the best photograph and theme it (for things like the view, animals, sunsets, etc.) during the hiking trip. Nature is free, and many of these trails have cheap camping sites nearby.

We don't cycle. It's not our thing. If it's your thing (and you don't yet have bikes) remember to keep an eye out for garage/yard sales and secondhand stores, online sites, etc. Go on Facebook or advertise on a community page that you are looking to find some bikes and helmets for the kids. You would be surprised how many people give away bikes and helmets. Most often, these items are sitting in their garage not being used, perhaps because those families have grown children now.

The fitness aspect of camping, hiking, and biking cannot be ignored. A genuine appreciation for the environment and our responsibility to it can be developed from an early age with these activities. Remember, pack your home-made delicious picnic and take your re-usable water bottles. Oh, and sunscreen and bug spray, purchased during a half-price sale of course.

Returning to Outside Family and Friends Fun

In terms of scenario planning, I would deem returning to family fun outside as a critical uncertainty. By this I mean it will be dependent upon social distancing, flattening

Chapter 3: Cheap Family Entertainment and Gifts

the curve, or even eradication. You will find outdoor family fun locally, but it may be very different.

When community events are scheduled again as restrictions for COVID-19 are lifted, check your local noticeboards, free newspapers, online events, and local museums/historical societies to see what's free and when. Exercise social distancing as part of your fun. When planning, write on a whiteboard in the kitchen "what's on when" and plan accordingly where to go and what to do safely. Eventually, concerts and music events will return. You never know who is going to be the "next big thing" at the free concert in the park. A few years ago, there was a free busking competition in our local park featuring a great singer with a cool vibe and terrific tunes. Lots of people loved this performer and met her, took selfies with her, and congratulated her after she won the competition. Tones and I then released a funky, famous tune titled *Dance Monkey*.

Gig guides often have many free musical events. Also, check out and search online for arts and crafts in your area. So many artists are online looking to cheer us up from lounge rooms around the world. When sports resume, do not worry if you cannot afford to go to a big-name sporting event. Be clever and go and see the juniors play and follow a "soon to be sporting legend" from the beginning of their journey. Enter competitions for events yourself if you can; you will be surprised how many you can win. Our friends previously have won everything from donuts to business class airfare, and even *meet and greets* with famous musicians like Adam Lambert and Queen. There is a saying: you have to be in it to win it!

Chapter 4: Cheap Shopping Tips

COVID-19 has affected us all. External factors have significantly impacted businesses and now the home front. One of our key coping factors was to reduce grocery, utility, and clothing costs. This aspect of scenario planning, concerning external factors, has now changed how we live and shop. Maybe for some, just going shopping is like an experience in an apocalyptic film or TV show. Slowly, our lives are beginning to return back to the way they were before.

Some of these scenario planning tips may seem obvious now in retrospect. Honestly though, it wasn't until I started doing them that I realized how wasteful I had been. If you are already doing some of these, well done! You are on your way to saving lots of money. If not, I challenge you to try them for one month. Calculate how much you save. Changing your shopping patterns is one of the biggest potential savers. With COVID-19, that has meant we have all had to quickly adapt. Use this revelation as a future motivator. What you do with the savings is the other motivator. Here are a few tips and suggestions to alter your bad shopping patterns and start living more cheaply.

Go Organic at Home and Grow a Basic Garden

No doubt many of you are doing this already during COVID. However, let me be the first to tell you that I was famous for killing every plant I ever attempted to grow before I started living cheaply. At least, until I planted my own garden.

I'm going to let you in on a little secret. Shhhh. By planting, I mean that I went to Bunnings and purchased already grown herbs, tomatoes, and lettuces. Even now during COVID times Bunnings is considered essential shopping. I brought them home. They sit on the verandah. I water them every day. During summer here in Australia where we live, sometimes we get bugs. No problem. I place a netted food cover over them and water them through that. That's it. Thankyou Bunnings.

If (unlike me) you can grow a plant, do it! If not, choose any store that has pre-planted herbs. I use them every day. It saves me about 15-20% off my weekly shopping bill. You will see exactly how a little further on, in Chapter 5

Cheap Easy Meals to Make. We always follow this process now, and it was especially helpful in preparation for lock down.

Plan Your Shopping Trip

1. Look inside your fridge, freezer and cupboards. What do you already have? What do you need?

2. Meal plan with what you already have. This is so important. You can reduce your shopping bill almost by half if you effectively meal-plan. We plan for a month. It's easy. We have a small whiteboard in the kitchen where we map out the family favorites week by week. The kids can write requests. It only takes a little time and if you do it well once, from then on you will always know what to buy. If you're unsure what that might look like, check out our *Monthly Meal Plan*. Oh, and the suggested shopping list.

3. Make a list. Whether it's the old-fashioned way on paper or through Alexa, your list actually saves you a lot of money. Shop only once a week. This also reduces car expenses like fuel and wear and tear, in addition to impulse spending. How interesting that during COVID times this became the norm!

4. Shop online. You can still use coupons and buy discounted items.

5. Always check for specials.

Meal Planning, and Save by Buying in bulk

Australia finally caught up with the rest of the world about 5 years ago when one of my favorite shops, Costco, arrived. In fact, I should send them a thank you basket after every holiday we take because without buying in bulk we wouldn't save anywhere near as much money. Wholesale stores have enabled us to save both time and money. Buying in bulk is cheaper than buying individual items.

A question I am often asked is, "What if I don't have enough spare cash to buy in bulk?" The answer is you do. Sometimes our freezers, cupboards, and fridges have enough ingredients that if forced to, you could manage to scrape together some basic meals. No doubt you have started to be highly skilled at this during lockdown. My advice is to do what we did, with whatever you have.

At the beginning of our "living more cheaply" journey we had rice, generic pasta, tinned tomatoes, spices, tinned soups, a taco kit, tuna, and two-minute noodles in the cupboard. We had one packet of mince (ground beef) along with some sausages and frozen vegetables in the freezer. In the fridge we had two onions, some potatoes, sliced cheese, lettuce, and a handful of carrots. We were really living on the edge, and there wasn't much else left in the house. I realized quickly that unless we changed our habits and taught ourselves better food management we wouldn't be able to feed ourselves, let alone raise the kids who lived with us. We had to use up everything we had so we could buy more cheaply on the next shop. And to be honest, I was terrified. I didn't know how I was going to stretch it. Maybe you have experienced the same feelings during the crisis?

You can eat cheaply, too, especially now during COVID times, by stocking your fridge, freezer, and cupboard with what I mentioned above. I managed to create some really yummy meals like pea risotto, vegetable pasta, soup night, tuna pasta bake, spaghetti Bolognese, and a taco night. I only bought milk, bread, cheese, and eggs, because I worked out that if I only spent $10, then I would have $90 each week to save for a bulk shop. With careful meal planning we had more than enough for two weeks with some of our staples (like flour) left over, too.

I suggest for your first two weeks to meal plan with only what is currently left in your fridge, freezer, and pantry with a few dollars aside for top-up items like we did. Then allocate what you would normally spend on your weekly shop. At the back of this book I have included a list of the meals we regularly cook on our monthly meal plan. I wanted to write about it in order to teach others how to live cheaply, too. I wrote it during the period just after COVID-19 took over the world – but when editing it before publication, I realized many of the tips I shared "for life as we knew it" will be essential moving forward. I thought what would help me the most was a list of meals that I could cook which were nutritious and cost-saving, all on one list. So now it is yours. There will be more cheap meal ideas in my upcoming *You Can Slow-Cook Cheaply Too During and After COVID-19* series. Hopefully, the inclusion of the meals in the appendices will help you minimize the amount of time you would have spent on narrowing down affordable meals, similar to the process of *scenario logic* – often the hardest part of settling on decisions.

Chapter 4: Cheap Shopping Tips

Forget Expensive Labels

The best thing we did to live cheaply was to buy generic and only buy things on special. It's the simplest way to live cheaper, especially now as we move forward. Many supermarkets are focusing on their own brands; from Woolworths and Coles (Australia), Walmart and Costco (USA), to Sainsbury, Tesco (UK), Picard and Carrefour in Europe, all retailers who provide almost all necessary staples for a well-stocked pantry and fridge/freezer at half the cost of brand labels. You can halve your weekly shopping bill automatically just from buying generic. Of course, sometimes the label "specials" are cheaper. You don't have to miss out on those things, just buy them on sale. Many friends whine to me, "But I only like that label." They are often shocked when I explain to them those products and generic versions almost always come from the same company and manufacturing plant. Often, the only difference is that the conveyor belt is stopped and the generic label replaces the label on the company product. Seriously. I like to remind myself of the question of, "Who is the clever shopper – the person paying extra for the label or the person paying for the same product at half the cost?" Win-win!

Strategizing – Sourcing Discounts, Specials, and Coupons

There are always local and weekly specials. Trusty coupons are still very easy to find and can save you hundreds of dollars each week on common household items as well. You only need 5-10 minutes a week to look for specials. Now, as we slowly return to normal from COVID-19, there will be re-opening specials and savings incentives galore. Remember to always look for online coupons and for those in your weekly paper to download or cut for use on the next shopping trip. These savings add up considerably. One of the best things to stock up on when discounted are your staples such as flour, sugar, tea, coffee, treats, frozen items, cleaning supplies, toilet paper, and feminine hygiene products. Where possible buy them in bulk, even if you are single. Spread over the month and year, bulk purchases can help save hundreds and even thousands.

We freeze everything, including flour and cake mixes. We had a house full of 3 teenage girls for two years. I saved $700 per teenager each year buying their personal hygiene products in bulk. We then used that money to do a cheap trip around New Zealand. Well worth it.

Saving at the checkout counter means your savings start to build. Then you can plan for affordable luxuries. Prior to COVID-19, we purchased luxury items, went on cruises, road trips, to theme parks, overseas holidays, and even flew business class – cheaply. I'm here to teach you how you can, too, even after COVID. A year or so after this crisis ends travel will be high on the list. Every day at dinner we imagine where we are eating (when COVID-19 is over) with our savings and planning how to do it once that magical activity is available again.

Shop in Your Pajamas Online

When we are time-poor, we waste money on pre-packaged expensive foods and impulse buying. During COVID times we are all managing time carefully. Between working from home, meal planning, online learning and home schooling, time is very important. To avoid the pre-packaged trap, sometimes I have shopped online during my lunch break at work or when at home. In the past I have shopped while waiting to pick-up the kids from sports and dance class. All right, sometimes I may have sneaked into the dance class and joined in, but most of the time I buy online specials to be delivered to my front door. There's no need for my car, my petrol, and my tires to be used all the time, saving me extra money across the year. Think about how much you have saved on these things during lockdown. Try and remember that when things get back to normal.

I often buy online items cheaper than in the store. This also helps me avoid impulse buys. I know how hard it is to resist an impulse purchase, so when I think I am going to cave I ask myself, 'Is it on the shopping list?" Even during COVID I have wanted to impulse purchase. Yesterday, I saw my makeup offered at half-price. If it isn't on the list, then it isn't a necessity. My impulse buys are significantly reduced. Of course, there will be times when a treat is on special and I might impulse buy, but only if it can be frozen or if it's half price!

You can plan successful shopping scenarios cheaply. Using these tips will greatly help you to save money. Now, read on to learn how you can prepare cheap meals easily.

Chapter 5: Cheap Easy Meals to Make

Prior to COVID-19, once I had started to save money on the weekly shops I invested in a small additional freezer in the garage and stocked up on frozen foods. I recommend this as a strategy going forward, too. It helped to plan ahead for not only a month, but those times when we were tired after work with no energy to cook from scratch. We realized we needed to spend money to save money here. The freezer purchase meant I could just reach in and have a homemade ready meal to go. You will be surprised at how much you save with this system. Resisting the urge to waste money constantly on takeout became very easy, especially as I became more organized. With COVID-19 this has been an even more invaluable tool. I have made Indian Curries in bulk to freeze in containers so that once a week we can feel like it is a take-away night.

Let's take a look at how to create further savings when planning meals. The meals listed at the end of the book are what I wish I had when I started to live and shop cheaply. I hope they help you during COVID-19 and after.

Buying Fresh Meat to Cook and Freeze

The price of meat can be expensive, but there are some tricks I'd like to share with you. I always disliked going through the meat aisle – and not because I once was a vegan, but because I am always shocked by the prices. I find the following options help reduce costs.

1. Buy meat in bulk. Buying in bulk is your best friend in the meat cooking department. Many local butchers will offer meat packs and specials. When meal planning, aim to have a variety of different protein dishes each week. The cuts of meat don't have to be expensive, and you will be surprised how far it can stretch with easy additives like frozen vegetables and other side dishes.

2. Decide what you are going to cook for the first two nights of your weekly shop.

3. On each of those nights, cook twice the amount you need. Eat one lot, freeze the other. This way when you are tired, and not wanting to cook, you can defrost one and have an amazing meal another night during the monthly meal plan.

4. Freeze the different meats you have bought in reasonable portion sizes and easy to reuse containers, and label them. Labelling your frozen goods (with the date you put them in the freezer) makes it easier to find things in the freezer and plan for weekly meals.

With those first savings we earned from meat shopping and cooking cheaply, I invested in a small deep freezer.

Great COVID-19 Bulk Buys

Furthermore, buying meat like ground beef, pork, chicken, and turkey mince is a huge cost saver. We also often buy a whole ham when on sale, and it makes us many a yummy meal. We section it when we buy it. One quarter is for an oven roasted meal that night, one quarter sliced for sandwiches, which can also be frozen. Even though schooling is from home at the current time, I encourage the kids to come in the kitchen and make ham and cheese sandwiches (like we do in normal times) which can be frozen for both school lunches and home family movie night (when one of our favorites is to "have a toastie").

Everyone loves a cheesy ham toasted sandwich! I dice the third quarter of the ham and freeze it in smaller bags or containers for when I like to make carbonara pastas. The last section of the ham is the bone with meat left on. Of course, on day 2, it goes in the slow cooker for pea and ham soup.

Another go-to for the weekly shop is store-cooked whole hot chicken. We buy a pre-cooked hot chicken on a Sunday night. Very strategic. We eat the legs and wings and some breast meat. I shred the rest and use it to make *chicken and cheese wraps* for the kids' lunches. We live in a hot climate, so we freeze wraps and sandwiches, which also makes the school run in the morning easy as lunch is already made. Now while working from home during COVID, I have the kids in school hour routines, such as breaks for morning tea and lunch when they are home. They reach into the freezer and grab the school lunch for "play time."

On school days the kids can also take a small container of salad to add to their wrap or sandwich. There aren't school lunch programs in Australia, so organization and nutrition is important. Now with SARS-CoV-2, the Coronavirus strand which causes COVID-19, this strategy should help those of you at home with your families. We have found keeping a routine in place invaluable to maintaining organization and a healthy mindset. I have even scheduled an extra learning activity for

Chapter 5: Cheap Easy Meals to Make

home economics where the eldest, who is an amazing baker, bakes our cake mixes. We then grade the cakes on a scale of 1-10.

Invest in a Slow Cooker

Perhaps this advice should be listed first and foremost. With a slow cooker you can make any meal cheaply, nutritiously, and full of flavor. Any cheap cut of meat becomes tasty in one of these. I often buy cheaper steak and dice it or de-bone chicken thighs and dice. Chicken tenders and fillets when they are on sale always go in the trolley. What I love about the butchers compared to the grocery store is that if you ask, they will often slice and dice for you. Get to know the butcher. Not like in an "Alice and Sam the butcher" way from The Brady Bunch, but instead in a "supporting local businesses" way. Essential shopping during COVID has enabled us to avoid crowds while supporting local small businesses who need us.

It's easy to make curry, casseroles, sauces for pasta, and about a hundred other things with your slow cooker. I even cook Bolognese and carbonara sauces in it! Meals in a slow cooker take less than 15 minutes in the morning before work to get ready and turn on. It is so nice to be at work and know dinner is already ready. (Of course, during COVID-19 the commute from the kitchen to the lounge room for work is so strenuous!)

I also use the slow cooker for soups. Soup bones are cheap, and when in the slow cooker all day with some herbs from your garden, garlic, onion, and stock cubes, the broth can be used for many different meal bases. After you strain your broth to remove bones, it can also be frozen for future usages. One day a month the fresh soup bones create enough base for 4-5 soups, and I also use it as the stock base for my Bolognese sauce and some of my curries.

I also have been making chicken and noodle broth during COVID from $1 packet soups. Delicious and hearty!

Become the Leftover Repurposing Food Expert with Stretch Meals

Leftovers are my go-to for budgeting hacks, nights when I can't stand wasting food, and when I am lazy. Everyone gets lazy with cooking. Your meal planning skills can really be utilized here. When I am tired of cooking, I immediately get out my slow cooker. In goes soup or a curry base. I add frozen or fresh vegetables which need to be used up so they don't go waste. Tinned coconut milk or cream is an essential item, as it's great for Thai soups or curries.

Repurposing food from its original incarnation is, actually, a very rewarding experience. Everyone in our house knows after spaghetti Bolognese night is taco night. Pretty easy to re-heat your Bolognese sauce with a taco kit sachet and have taco meat. These "stretch meals" really help the budget. I sneak in frozen or tin corn and beans whenever I can, too.

Many children who have lived with us over the years don't like vegetables, and some have tragically never even tasted them before – this is, sadly, normal for the life of some foster kids. I often grate carrot and zucchini to hide it in stretch meals. I have even grated raw beetroot to red sauce dishes. My repurposing hacks include turning leftover Bolognese sauce into an Asian based curry San Choy Bau. Just add 1-2 tablespoon of yellow curry powder, 1 tablespoon of mustard powder, 1 tablespoon of soy sauce, 1 diced onion, 2 cups of water and some sultanas while reheating. Serve it in lettuce leaves from your garden. On these stretch meal nights with an Asian twist, I serve a fortune cookie for dessert. The kids love it and get so excited. We use this as an opportunity to talk about our future travel dreams which correspond to the table fare. Think Mexico, Asia, Greece and you get the idea. COVID-19 is not stopping our dreams; it's just pausing them for a little while!

Portion, Make, and Freeze Desserts

Lots of people are going to tell you that home baking is cheaper than buying baked goods. And yes, that is mostly the case. Having flour in your cupboard is a must, not just for cakes but for savory cooking, too. You can make cakes, pikelets, pancakes, scones, and biscuits all from scratch – but, if you're like me and your baking isn't the best, you aren't going to break your budget by buying a cake mix. Most local supermarkets have a generic brand of vanilla and chocolate cake mixes.

In Australia, the cheapest of these is 80 cents. You know what I'm talking about here ... the "add water and stir" mixes; just bake, add icing, and you have an inexpensive cake for school lunch boxes, parties, and desserts. These are extremely affordable when you bake them in a square or rectangular tray because you can slice and freeze the cake for school lunches besides enjoying the fresh cake for a few days after baking. Icing is easy. Icing sugar is so cheap. Lazy, like me? Time poor? You can use a tea strainer and just sprinkle the icing/sugar powder onto the cake, or mix it

Chapter 5: Cheap Easy Meals to Make

with some butter and vanilla essence (or coco powder).

I bet you are thinking, "Who has the time to bake during COVID-19?" I'll tell you who: the kids! In normal times (when they return – and they will return) it's still going to be the teenager – she just doesn't realize it yet! You will also have time to do it, especially on hot whole cooked chicken night. I often get the kids to stir the cake mix the old-fashioned way, with a wooden spoon. Whoever stirs the best batch gets to lick the spoon. Incentives like this can be early indicators that the homemade dessert is appreciated!

If you don't enjoy baking and don't have kids, I often find specials at the supermarket where whole cakes are on sale for half-price or even less. I buy these up big time. I portion control them, cut, slice, and freeze them. Portion control has meant my weight has stayed the same during COVID. Asking when the store normally discounts those items is a good idea so you can shop at mark-down time. Obviously, this applies to all your grocery items, too. If it's less than half-price, buy it! Check out Facebook for some really great local pages on markdowns in your area. Yes, they are still happening even during COVID-19 times.

Staples and Cupboard Essentials are a Must

Always have staples like flour, baking powder, spices, and stock cubes in your cupboard. This is a living cheaply essential! Buy tinned tomatoes, corn, and pulses like chickpeas, black beans, lentil soup mix, beetroot, tuna, and salmon. Buy generic pasta, as most cost less than $1 per packet. Buy them in a variety of shapes and types like spirals, bow tie, macaroni, spaghetti, fettucine, and gnocchi. I have some gorgeous spaghetti canisters where I store my pastas and they are on display in the kitchen for décor. My meal list at the back of the book will help you learn how cheaply you can cook with these staples.

Eat Out Once a Week

Notice I said eat out. It doesn't have to be at a restaurant, as long as you are out of the house. During COVID times this could be in your garden or by a pool. As restrictions are relaxed, consider other outside venues again. A BBQ by a lake, a park, or beach can be a great way to eat out cheaply. When we can socialize again, talk to your friends about a pot-luck night and take it in turns to host one even once a month. Plan a picnic and theme it; for example one where everyone wears white clothing and brings different types of sandwiches and home-made cakes.

Eating somewhere other than in your house at least once week is the aim. This is a surprisingly achievable, fun way to enjoy dinner out. Sure, you can find a cheap take-out or go to a cheap restaurant as things reopen. Most restaurants will return to offering cheaper specials on Mondays and Tuesdays. A lot of our local Mexican restaurants, for example, offer 50 cent wings nights and $1 tacos, and have even done so during COVID-19. Look for "buy one get one free" specials and keep an eye out for other deals. If you are saving for something else, still plan to eat out but do it cleverly, perhaps by sometimes taking your food to go if it means a cheaper bill. Enter competitions to win dinners and gift vouchers.

Sign up to free memberships which give discounts and perks. Go to restaurants that have loyalty rewards such as making the 5th or 10th meal free. Download apps like *Groupon*, *Scoopon*, *The Fork*, and *First Table*. You can still dine out to enjoy a break and change of pace for a cheap price.

Chapter 6: Clothing Cheaply and Stylishly After COVID-19

I had a professional day job for 25 years where I had to be dressed perfectly (and stylishly) every day. I also had a second job where my business partner and I ran a successful catering business at music festivals. From the very beginning of my career I had to quickly learn how to dress fashionably and affordably for the day job and "mix and match" for the catering gigs. I wore a mix of designer and K-mart. I loved our catering gigs the most because jeans and shirts were the standard. You can dress cheaply with flare.

As foster carers, clothing the kids who lived with us was made easy and cheap thanks to some simple organization techniques and a sensible yearly budget. Most importantly, we focus on sustainable clothing. None of us like the idea of negatively contributing to the environment, and I admit I really love the fact Hollywood finally caught up and made vintage (secondhand clothing) trendy and sustainable.

During COVID times, I readily admit I have worn pajama bottoms and a dress shirt for video conferencing. When things return to normal I will be ready, as I have spent time organizing the clothes I already have, an essential clothing strategy – particularly for the kids. I find that by hanging and folding clothes in different categories in the wardrobes it becomes easy to allocate work clothes, going out clothes (dinner, date, wedding/special occasions church etc.), and school clothes. I follow the exact same process for the grown-ups. Surprisingly, I find that with pre-planned mix and matching that I can turn 10 pieces of clothing into many different outfits. I use the same method even when we travel. More on that later. Yes, we are planning to travel.

Only Buy New When On Sale

I love Xmas sales, Black Friday sales – any sales, really. I have become an expert at finding items on sale. Remember to buy only what you need or know you will need in advance. Kids grow quickly, so habitually buying one to two sizes up from what they are currently wearing means you can get great discounts. About a month before COVID, I knew that the designer store I loved was having a clearance rack with $2 shirts and $7 swimwear. Many stores will have clothes marked down to even 95% off. Don't forget to check online, too. My kids love it when Calvin Klein is on sale at Costco, but they love it even more when we find it somewhere unexpected. If vintage shopping isn't your thing, and my argument of sustainability isn't appealing, you can still shop designer brand names without the outrageously high price tags typical of big department stores.

You can find so many $1 clothing sales online. OK. I want you to stop reading one minute from now. Use your search engine and type in "$1 clothing sales" or your equivalent currency. Try only buying new each season when items are on sale. So many retailers are online during COVID-19 and there are sales, sales, and more sales. If you can afford to, buy some bargains and help them. Ready to shop from the comfort of your pajamas?

Organization is the Key with Storage

This is such a handy tip for any parent/carer. Storage bins help teach kids not only to be clean and tidy, but how to classify, categorize, and be organized. These skills then carry on into school, too. For example, in Mathematics, Geography, and Science, classification and graphing are intrinsic procedures. The kids don't even realize they are constantly developing these skills while they are folding their clothes and returning them after washing. Colored bins are great, especially if your kids are sharing a room. When they grow out of clothes, of course, the clothes can be used by the next child, or given to a friend or family member, or even the local secondhand shop.

I also keep an eye out on the next size up the kids are about to go to while shopping for clothes. While *Miss 15* is doing her *vintage challenge*, I keep an eye out for other bargains that kids can grow into as well as for stuff for me and the hubby. Almost always, I find designer and name brand clothing – most even literally with the price tag still on them. I have found Dior, Vera Wang, Ralph Lauren and items from Zara, Osh Kosh, Pumpkin Patch, Bonds, and countless others. Miss 15 often would spot things for me, too, at a dramatically low price! She would then cheekily suggest where she would like to go on holiday next with us from the savings! Her online vintage challenge is morphing into a "what she would like to find" list when she is able to go to a store again.

Chapter 6: Clothing Cheaply and Stylishly After COVID-19

School vs. Sand

We are fortunate to live near a beach, but sand is my enemy. Everything ends up with sand in it everywhere, and by everywhere I mean *everywhere!* During COVID-19 we have been lucky and can leave the house for essential exercise on the beach. Sun, sand, saltwater, mud, and grass always end up entrenched on the kids' clothes. How do we save money here? Easy. I make them change out of school uniforms or their school clothes before play. Normally on weekends, it's the "no playtime until after breakfast and chores are finished" rule. During online learning it is a "no play until school work is finished" rule (plus one extra household chore completed). Then they change into play clothes. The kids also know the rules; if it's dirty or stained they put the outfit straight in the laundry tub for soaking. If something has a rip or tear, they sit with me and we repair it together.

Good clothes that are well-worn become play-clothes, but I have also regularly found both "going out" and play clothes like shirts, shorts, and pants for as cheap as $0.50 per item in secondhand stores. I always emphasize the importance of sustainability with clothing. We once had a teenager who lived with us who only liked designer clothes, a bad habit from her previous foster parents. I sat her down and showed her a YouTube video of how much clothing is wasted every year around the world, and the working conditions of the factories, in order to "de-consumerise" her. It worked. I then offered her an incentive. I gave her the "Rogers-Jones Vintage Shopping Challenge."

It goes like this. Once a month I would take her to the secondhand store and give her $15. She was amazed at how many different items she could mix and match with what she had at home. From clothing, belts, and jewelry, she gave "vintage chic" a whole new meaning. It was also a really nice time once a month when it was just her and me to bond and help her heal and move forward with her life. Her formal outfit was so beautiful; a vintage bridesmaid dress which we repurposed. We got out the trusty glue gun and sequined with crystals and motifs. Stunning! Our current teenager has an online vintage challenge and is doing really well with it.

During COVID times, mail delivery is still working well in Australia. Of course, all COVID-19 sanitation precautions are taken when clothing arrives.

Chapter 6: Clothing Cheaply and Stylishly After COVID-19

Donated New Goods to Secondhand Stores

When retail and furniture stores are overstocked and need to make room for new inventory once their sales have finished, they often donate surplus stock to local secondhand stores. Just before COVID lockdowns, our local store recently donated hundreds of mattresses which the bedding company had an oversupply of. We took our savings and replaced our bedding as required. Other times we have also found crockery, cutlery, towels, sheets, and duvets – all new – which we purchased for a fraction of the retail price.

I would daresay that with COVID-19 when stores open, there will be many bargains and many vintage clothing options. Don't think of this as being a bad thing to do (looking for a cheap price), instead remind yourself that you are helping businesses get back on their feet and saving landfill. Many people also find bargains at discount wholesalers and department stores.

Build your vintage, environmentally repurposed wardrobe via sales and clearance racks and you and your family will always be clothed and housed sustainably, stylishly, and cheaply. If you are thinking or feeling embarrassed that you are living cheaply, stop feeling that way now! There is no reason whatsoever why you should feel that way. In fact, you should feel the opposite. Remind yourself that you are living a sustainable lifestyle and reducing your carbon footprint.

How are people going to know where you purchased clothing unless you tell them? And when you do tell them, be proud. Tell them and show them by example how to live more cheaply. Ask yourself who is the winner here? The person who pays more for the same lifestyle or the person who pays less? Who is the person helping the environment the most? You! Besides, with COVID times comes a shared experience of living affordably.

Chapter 7: Cheaper Travel – Scenario Planning for the Unknown

The one scenario I correctly anticipated from the impact COVID-19 was how it would destroy our travel plans – albeit temporarily. Remember it's only a pause, not a stop! We were booked for the European family trip of our lifetime in April to visit some of the kids who have lived with us over the years. We cancelled in the first week of February. We were able to easily foresee that what had started in northern Italy would be the case around the world in only a matter of weeks. So, we cancelled the trip and were refunded in full. When the world recovers, so too will our desire to travel again – probably more than ever.

By the time international travel fully opens up again to the way it once was, I forecast it will most likely be 2-3 years from now. Scenario planning in terms of narratives comes to play here when thinking about future travel. We now spend every meal at night saying where in the world we are eating, with the view to going there one day. So, obviously, taking into account our living cheaply skills, we can use our significant savings to treat ourselves to a luxurious holiday in the future when COVID-safe travel starts up. By the time we fly again to Italy it will be in first class with a shower in the sky – all right, maybe business class. No, definitely First Class with our extra savings! YOLO.

I have put together travelling tips from before and for after COVID-19 to help you plan your next long-awaited travel adventure. Before COVID, we always sourced excellent deals. I'd like you to read these tips and remember them, as once things get back to normal there will be bargains everywhere to tap into to get local, interstate, and worldwide travel back up and running.

Prior to COVID-19, I could easily tell you that you can holiday cheaply anywhere if you know the secrets to affordable luxury travel. In fact, for our original trip in April, we secured our first-class tickets with our rewards points from our credit cards and weekly shopping saved over the previous three years. Living cheaply means you are saving money now during COVID and after. A great example prior is our "left the nest 20 somethings" who were always going somewhere around the world with their

Chapter 7: Cheaper Travel

friends because they have been taught how to implement (and use to their advantage) everything I am sharing with you.

The teens at home are learning from them, too, by planning trips for when COVID-19 is over. You should see them hacking their ideas, albeit with a little jealousy that they aren't quite that age or able to do it just yet because of COVID-19. When things do open up, there will be many deals. Airlines around the world have fuel stored, and there is already talk of reduced domestic airfares so airlines can use up those resources. Even if international travel is slower to start at this stage, domestic deals will be plentiful. Follow your country's COVID-safety travel advice in planning, and make your decision from there if you wish to fly or cruise.

Of course, only travel if it's safe. Whether you are single or wanting to experience a wholesome family fun vacation, many of the tips below may not be what you are accustomed to – but I promise that you will see the savings you will earn by using these tips compared to previous travel habits you may have had in the past. I think we will all be surprised just how much we will appreciate travel as a living cheaply goal after COVID times.

Domestic Travel in COVID Times by Bus and Train

Before making travel plans always check for specials. During and following COVID local travel will be the first to open up, making train and bus a great choice. At the time of this writing, the companies I refer to here for deals remain solvent. Many bus and train specials pop up all the time. In the UK, for example, National Express often offers "one-pound deals" for internal travel in the UK – and during peak season, if you purchase in advance, 5 pound fares. In the past we have timed our trips to the UK to see family when these bus specials are on, as they are much cheaper than a hired car and we get to relax and enjoy the scenery. In Australia, America, and Canada, Greyhound services run almost over these entire countries in air-conditioned comfort and with free wifi in most. You can even buy a yearly pass and take as many unlimited trips as you like.

Look out for sales coming up on all forms of domestic travel. I suspect forward bookings and sales to re-establish capital will happen to encourage tourism, thus making domestic travel extremely affordable. Other local and interstate USA and Canadian companies include Megabus, Boltbus, Lux Bus, and Red

Chapter 7: Cheaper Travel

Coach. After the pandemic, many of these businesses can hopefully stay afloat. One thing is certain: the way to help that is to plan and book trips, maintaining social-distancing as required and keeping with hygienic habits. Countries will need to rebuild local tourism first. So, bus and train are going to be easy, enjoyable, and priced to get tourists back on seats and to destinations safely.

Taking the train is also a great way to holiday and see any country. Train fares are always on sale. This is where you can wisely manage your hard-saved dollars. We have jagged so many cheap train fares internally in the UK and Europe, some as little as $10 from one country to another. In America we have also saved on train fares. We drive on the other side of the road in Australia, so as much as we would love to drive cross-country on USA Route 66, we have decided to take the train on our "after-COVID trip" to visit family and friends. It is a much better and cheaper option! Thank you, Amtrak. Social-distancing on a train is easier than on a plane, so start planning some train travel. Try and book overnight journeys, as you save on the cost of a hotel for those nights and wake up fresh in your destination.

Hotel Memberships, Subscriptions, and Clubs

There are some amazing memberships out there, and they are easy to find and subscribe to online. Best Western, Hilton, and Accor offer discounts and incentives. ALL (the Accor Live Limitless program) has great deals. Many of these companies have ensured that their members can use their benefits when travel begins again. Throughout the year they offer half-price sales on their accommodations all over the world. We often get hotels like the Sofitel, Novotel, Mecure, and their entire hotel range for 50% off. They also have a paid membership scheme in Australia, Asia, and the South Pacific regions.

As an Accor Plus member you receive one free night's accommodation at any resort/hotel in that area, half-price dining at their restaurants (even if you aren't staying on site), access to yearly half-price sales, and in Asia 15-25% off your drinks. If you live in any of those countries (or are travelling to any) the cost of the card is recouped after you use your free night. For example, the card cost me $395 for the yearly fee. I used my free night at the stunning Sofitel Darling Harbor which normally costs $700@ per night. So, not only did I make my money back on the card in this

Chapter 7: Cheaper Travel

expensive hotel, I stayed somewhere I would never be able to afford at full price. I also booked an extra two nights on their half-price member's sale, too, and had a terrific long weekend in Sydney.

As a member that gave us all a free buffet breakfast, too. Meeting Will Smith's son Jayden in the foyer as he was leaving was just an added bonus! One of the best things about the ALL product is you earn points along the way which can be used to pay for rooms, dining, or are even transferable to a frequent flyer program. You also have tiers; we are currently Platinum which means free Executive Club access at any Accor property throughout the world that has an executive club. So that means free breakfast, free drinks, and canapes and refreshments all day for us and the kids!

Friends in the USA swear by their Hilton membership because of its tier structure, too. I highly encourage you to take the time to research online for free sign-up based membership programs, or a paid membership that you can afford. The thing I like about our Accor Plus is that we do not have to spend extra on food.

During COVID they have really looked after members and extended their memberships free of charge for 6 months, so that we can still access their benefits when travel reopens. We already know that as soon as we can go to a hotel within driving distance, we are taking the kids to enjoy somewhere that isn't home! The kids love the buffet and breakfast options, and the canapes and nibbles at night are more than enough for dinner. Some of the hotels also do chocolate buffets and desert buffets. The Movenpick resorts are great for the afternoon teas. If you add up how much you would spend even on your BYO camping food and drinks, the cost of the yearly membership can be quite affordable averaged out across the year.

If being a subscriber or member for special deals and perks isn't your thing, try staying in local motels, pensions/guest houses, bed and breakfasts, Airbnbs and inns. Helping locals in your holiday destination can be such an amazing way to holiday. These self-catering options can be so cheap. They often offer discounts to repeat visitors, too. When COVID restrictions are relaxed, our local and driving-distance options are going to need us all to stay a night if we can. Their local businesses are going to need us to buy meals and souvenirs, and to participate in activities. Throughout Europe there are many quaint and cheap pensions, affordable chalets, and tourist standard hotels with both half-board and full-board options available, often near ski resorts and hiking trails.

When overseas travel opens up and you are planning your trip, be sure to research and find the best deals for these types of accommodations in the area you are planning to vacation. Previously, I have found ski chalets in Austria for as little as $55 per person per night including breakfast and dinner, and apres ski yummies and drinks! Deals will be there after COVID – you just have to look for them. If you are planning a trip in the Asia/Pacifica or Oceania regions, look at purchasing or joining Accor.

House-Sitting and House Swapping for Free

I can't promise that you will meet Jude Law, but this is a wonderful way to have an almost free vacation (except for travel expenses of course). After COVID, swapping or house sitting will be a refreshing change of scenery. You'd be surprised how many of these opportunities exist within only a couple of hours of most households by car, train, or bus. You'd also be surprised how many people overseas want trustworthy people to look after their homes and animals while they are away. If you are retired, please pay attention here. If you'd like to retire early and affordably, read on.

We have retired friends who are constantly booked to do house-sits throughout the world. Each year they rent out their own property and buy an around-the-world airfare cheaply for $1100@. They have 12 months to use their airfare, so they plan where they'd like to house-sit. They are members of some housesitting sites where they advertise their experience and services. Individual owners on the site then contact them directly to organize their sits accordingly. It's not uncommon for them to sit 3-4 months at a time. As huge animal lovers, they now have fur-children scattered throughout the world. They live rent/mortgage free, are bill free and fancy free. During COVID-19 they have still been able to stay in their sits, and in fact were able to organize additional sits for people who couldn't get back to their own countries.

Cheap Eats during and After COVID-19 when on Holidays

While planning your holiday or mini-break to take during or after the pandemic, there are a couple of different ways you can save money while eating on vacation. Whether you have self-catering accommodation or not, it is easy to enjoy a meal without a huge price tag. One of the biggest ways to save money on eating expenses is by bringing your own food purchased from a grocery store. Even if staying in a motel, you can easily bring reusable plastic bowls and have cereal, milk, and fruit. For a hot breakfast, most motels and campsites have camp kitchens or BBQs so bacon, eggs, and pancakes are easily achieved. You can make sandwiches in the room or tent and then toast on the BBQ. We often find accommodations at half-price or on sale, and aim to stay somewhere luxurious because we know we can cut back on eats in order to enjoy the luxury amenities.

Before departing on your trip, search online for breakfast specials at cafes, restaurants, and diners in the areas. If you are staying in a commercial hotel always book the room rate which includes breakfast. Download apps like *The Fork*, *Groupon*, and *First Table* which have up to 50% off meal specials. We often have purchased 50% off deals prior to leaving on vacation and have enjoyed many half-price meals. You can even ask the kids to search where you are going for any discounts and specials. On family internet night we ask the kids to tell us what they found and why they'd like to eat there. The most convincing argument wins!

But if you still want to treat your family to one night out, ask the locals where they like to eat. When we have self-catering accommodation, we tend to have every 2nd night as either a cheap pizza night or discount dinner out. We also go to the grocery store upon arrival and purchase breakfast staples and a cooked chicken for sandwiches and dinner for the kids while the hubby and I go out on date night on holiday. For the once-a-year special vacation, we of course book the half-price sale hotels of our ALL/Accor Plus program.

Old Tips for the New COVID International Travel World

Often the best part of a holiday can be the planning stages. I love finding a bargain. My friends don't bother with a travel agent, instead they come over for a coffee and we find the best deal together online. Now our coffee sessions are socially-distanced or conducted via video! We remind ourselves that "this too will pass." While it may seem that air travel is a long ways off still, remember time goes by quickly. Soon planes will be flying again and while it might not be the commercial airline you are used to, low cost carriers will be very affordable and a pleasant option. Many already have great pre-

Chapter 7: Cheaper Travel

COVID reviews, high safety ratings, and most of all will save you money!

I have a friend who only flies with one carrier because she wants points. Yes, of course collecting points is a great if you are travelling all the time, but if it's the occasional yearly holiday then loyalty needs to be forgotten about and instead bargains found! Airline food is sometimes notoriously horrible, so why would you focus on a full-service flight that includes a drink and a meal and pay more for it? Doesn't make sense to me. We time our short-haul flights after meal times, like early morning or after lunch (which are often not peak times, either). Also, flying late night can be a huge money saver. We often fly overnight and check into a cheap airport hotel, so when we start our holiday the next morning we are fresh and ready to pound the pavement.

Set a budget when searching for deals and be smart. Find the cheapest air fare which allows you to spend more money when you arrive at your destination! I want you to also remember that for the same cost as an economy fare with one airline you can often find business class deals with another to the same destination. Sure, it may not be your usual airline but does that matter? One of the best things we have found is to research the partner airlines of one you like. Often, they are cheaper.

An example of this is when we went to London a few years ago from Sydney. QANTAS are partners with Sri Lankan Airlines. In fact, they code share. We found a discount business class fare with Sri Lankan for the same price as the full price economy QANTAS fare. We weren't planning on going to the UK, but when that deal came up, we changed our travel plans from Canada to the UK and Europe. Another hint here is to just search for any special. Sometimes we only choose our destination after we have found the flight deals. It has meant we have been to destinations we never thought possible. Research other traveler reviews and if most of the feedback is favorable, a much more affordable trip awaits you.

Low cost airlines are a fantastic option. We have found fares as low as $30 including carry-on luggage with up to 23 kilograms within Europe. In the UK and Europe think Easy Jet, Ryan Air, Vueling, Eurowings, and, surprisingly, Lufthansa and British Airways. These all offer discount airfares in advance.

In America we have learned that Virgin, JetBlue, Delta, Southwest, Frontier, and Spirit are usually the cheapest with some fares as low as $15. In Australia join the Jetstar Club for discounted fares, plus Virgin Australia also always has fantastic discounted deals – hopefully they survive the pandemic. If you are organized and book in advance, you can find cross country fares for as little as $50 one way. The trick is to fly light. That's really easy because by now your wardrobe is "mixed and matched." For international flights (whether it's from the Pacific/Oceania or North America) you can't beat the Etihad, Virgin, Emirates, and Lufthansa fares. Often you can also book these flights for the end of the holidays or across the middle of the holiday period when prices are cheaper. We tend to fly when it isn't peak school holidays and leave a day or two earlier. As an ex-teacher I know that not much learning happens on those days. (Sorry, but it's the truth!)

COVID-19 - Holiday Local or Nearby Local by Road Tripping

I mentioned earlier, because of COVID-19 the first travel to open up will likely be domestic and local. The trusty tent and camping equipment is going to come in handy. With the fallout of the pandemic, road tripping becomes an obvious affordable holiday choice. We save money when road tripping by packing a cooler filled with drinks, snacks, sandwiches, cookies, and cakes. This makes the petrol/gas stop a lot cheaper. One pit-stop, if we were to pay for all those items, would cost our family $50-$60. That's insane! It's the cost of two nights camping at a full hook-up site. Whenever one of the kids might start to complain about the home brought goodies, I remind them that otherwise it means 2 less nights away. They soon learn not to ask when they know they are getting two extra days of holiday.

Before the road trip, have a look around for good discount petrol apps. There are many, so research as to where you can lock-in the price at its cheapest rate during the week. Plan your route, and then when you purchase your petrol later in the week you will only pay the price you locked in.

We have a rule when road tripping: we don't drive more than 2-3 hours a day. This way we see as much as possible, relax as much as possible, and experience as much as possible. Plus, the kids don't get on edge. The golden rule is one or two movies on the electronic device. The key in the past was organization and planning, now it is also local destinations first as the world recovers from isolation.

When international travel is safe again, and you are on a budget, you can save a lot of

Chapter 7: Cheaper Travel

money by buying lightweight camping gear when you arrive. Think tent, yoga mat, sleeping bag, and solar shower. I once bought a tent in Budapest for the equivalent of $35 and spent 3 months camping with four of us in Europe for less than $30 a night. So for $6 each per night we enjoyed camping by the Danube, the sights of Venice, the beach areas of the Cote d'azur, the Amalfi Coastline, the funky city of Berlin, wine regions in Burgundy, and waking up in the morning to snow covered tips of the Swiss Alps. By the way, that also included our food. We enjoyed pastas, baguettes, pancakes, BBQs, tacos, and anything that could be simply assembled and carried well to the next destination. We often ate local fruits and vegetables on the campfire roasted with spice rubs. Many times, we shared food and resources with fellow families out camping, too, and created many campfire feasts and magnificent memories. Someone almost always had a guitar so we enjoyed campfire singalongs. These wonderfully simple times will happen again.

Many local area museums and parks are very inexpensive to tour in Europe and can be booked in advance during your vacation time. When you take that dream trip a few years from now, remember that most European galleries and museums have one day a month where they have free entry, so scenario planning ahead is an easy way to save huge entrance fees (just be aware that those are the days with the longer lines).

Another thing to take into consideration is the time of year you plan to take your break from the "real world." It can be difficult right now to conceive the way the real world was, the world that currently is, and the world ahead when travel reopens. Given human nature, we will want to keep the good things like rituals, traditions, and history preserved all around the world, and we all need to see it at least once in our lives. Many cities that host famous attractions will lower their rates to encourage tourism. Not only will most of the attractions and events lower their rates, but most of the hotels and inns in your surrounding area will as well.

Another big benefit to touring a city during their off-season and recovery period is, of course, that there may be shorter lines to attractions and less traffic than during the high season. Yes, I believe we will have high and low seasons again. Yes, I believe we will travel again. Yes, I believe it will be affordable. Yes, there is hope.

Chapter 8: Cheap Living Constantly During and After COVID

There are many ideas herein that you can embrace. You don't have to incorporate all of them at once. Remember, slow and steady wins the race. Of course, sometimes you are going to over-indulge, especially when COVID-19 restrictions are lifted. I dream already of seeing our kids living overseas, flying again and in business class – make that first class! Dreams are important. Hope is important. Ironically, during this lockdown with little income, we have found a resourcefulness we didn't know we had. We have embodied everything I wrote about. I hope that by reading our experiences before and during COVID you have some takeaway ideas for after. If you can, try to keep a list on the fridge of your goals for what you want to do with your savings. Maybe some images of the places you'd like to go for a yearly holiday after COVID-19 and the world rebuilds. You could have a pin-board in the house and ask the kids to add photos of their goals and dreams. This helps greatly to motivate yourself and family to stay on track when rebuilding.

Always praise your family (or flatmates) for making better changes which save money and help the environment, especially those performed during this time of crisis that benefit everyone. Use this time to connect with family and enjoy simple things that inspire you to achieve things you couldn't beforehand. Teach each other to be responsible and make informed choices based on what you have available, and scenario plan for a better future.

Keep track of your monthly outgoings for a month before you start living in the real world again, after COVID-19. Then as the months go by, keep track and compare the savings. I can tell you, not only did we save a lot of money in the first 3-6 months simply by eliminating takeout and eating our prepared ready meals before the lockdowns, we have continued to do it now by circumstance. You have, too, most likely. This means you can continue it into the future.

Monitor your spending habits now from the crisis and the amounts of money going out of the household each month. Then each week as life starts to return to normal, maintain your food lists, menu planning, and most

Chapter 8: Cheap Living Constantly During and After COVID

importantly put your savings in a bank account without an ATM card. Yes, that's right, have one account that you don't have a card for. This is one of the best scenario planning strategies I can give you, an account without easy access to it for your savings. You won't spend it if you can't touch it!

This account also comes in handy for things like an unexpected trip to the doctor or pharmacy. At the end of the first 3 months of savings after transitioning back, treat yourself to something small and then save the rest until you reach the 6 month mark. That way you will always be 3 months ahead. COVID-19 has proven you never know what life will throw at you and at what time, so having the extra savings will help you be prepared for both emergencies and fun times ahead!

Once you've got your savings, enjoy them! You've changed your habits for a good reason and a good purpose, so be kind to yourself and treat yourself once in a while. Your new routines will automatically reduce debt in your life, allocate funds for early retirement, save for the kids' university expenses, and provide your dream holiday. You will find that living a better and healthier money-saving lifestyle has many benefits.

Give some serious thought to becoming a part-time energy wholesaler, or selling your favorite cosmetics, or distributing kitchenware for extra income. Perhaps you have a talent and can tutor people? Perhaps you have a story to tell? Perhaps you are a local who can offer a holiday experience through a platform like Airbnb?

Stuck for ideas? I have a book coming out soon about how to make passive income with an in-depth look at multiple scenarios you can choose from to prosper.

Further to the chapters here about shopping and cooking cheaply, my second book from the **You Can Too Motivation** series, *You Can Slow Cook Cheaply Too During and After Covid-19* will provide you with plenty of meal ideas and recipes, available from Amazon. Following that, I have timed the release of my third book *You Can Make Passive Income Too* to help people make money during and after the crisis.

I originally started this book during the pandemic. I really debated whether to publish it or not. Obviously, I didn't plan on there being a worldwide shutdown while I was writing it. However, it made me realize the unwavering relevance of the topic before COVID-19, during it, and now as we move forward with life after lockdown. The whole world has rapidly had to adjust to life with COVID-19, and I think we have all done a great job all things considered.

We have made stronger connections with our families, friends, and communities. The ozone is healing and planet earth is recovering. We have realized what is most important to us. We need to acknowledge that COVID-19 is going to be part of our lives for a very long time. But we can take what we have learned and continue to progress, and we can look forward to a better quality of life, more family time, and achieving our goals and dreams. You can live cheaply during and after COVID-19 too.

Camille

Appendices

Monthly Meal Plan List

Chicken, Ground Beef, or Pork Spaghetti Bolognese

Pasta Napolitana with basil

Tacos/Burritos – with tinned Mexican beans seasoned and/or meat

Lasagna – pre-bought or home made

Chicken Tender Caesar Salad

Chicken Cacciatore

Pizza night

Curries – Thai and Indian, meat and vegetarian

BBQ night

Vegetarian pasta fettucine

Tuna pasta bake, Vegetable pasta bake

Sandwich/Wrap night

Crumbed, battered, grilled, or steamed fish with chips and salad

Winter soups: Tomato and basil, Chicken and corn, Leftover beef and vegetable, Broth

Curried sausages or curried vegetables and rice

Filos/Pasties - Chicken and mushroom, Avocado cheese and bacon, Vegetable and cheese

Cooked chicken night – supermarket or home-cooked

Lemon-herbed baked chicken pieces

Risotto: Pea, Corn, Chicken and corn, Pumpkin, Frozen vegetable, Fish and cheese

Hot dogs

Side Dishes

Garlic bread

Cheesy herb garlic bread

Potato gratin

Vegetables, plain or gratin

Potato salad

Currie tuna pasta salad with raisins

Greek salad

Italian salad with bocconcini, basil, and tomato

Garden salad with grated cheese

Wok tossed vegetables

Frozen vegetables steamed

About the Author

Camille Rogers-Jones is a successful motivational writer and speaker who has, in truth, been motivating people she meets all her life – be it at work or in her personal life. The recipient of numerous Excellence in Teaching awards across her extensive 25-year teaching career, Camille thrives on improved learning outcomes for all students. She coached winning national sporting and dance eisteddfod teams, and has also led several curriculum initiatives to re-engage disengaged students. Subsequently, her behaviour management expertise with "at risk" kids became highly sought after.

Passionate about helping young people, Camille and her retired police officer husband have helped raise 25 children, many of whom have gone onto successful careers in fields such as medicine, architecture, international banking, fashion design, entrepreneurship, teaching, aeronautical engineering, and even a few television personalities.

Camille has regularly given presentations as a keynote speaker at educational conferences throughout Australia about the importance of arts and literacy education. And she loves to write about her amazing life experiences. Her genuine passion to mentor others shines through in her authentic, often humorous and "tell it like it is" style.

Camille also has a passion for cooking, and has run her own catering business for years – mostly at music festivals where she has met and cooked for many hungry musicians. Famous faces were regular around the home when artists on tour who were craving a home-cooked meal would drop by to dine, followed by a game of Pictionary. Serving vegan hotdogs to Dave Grohl and the Foo Fighters, poolside get-togethers with Michael Hutchence and his brother's family, enjoying home-made apricot chicken with Australian comedian Anthony Ackroyd and Upside Down comedy duo member David Collins; Camille cooked for some of the best during the 90's.

Yet she firmly believes that the most joyous times spent sharing meals have been with her large family. Since retiring from teaching and catering, Camille has transitioned to motivational writing and speaking. In her spare time Camille and her husband travel around the world visiting the beautiful children whose lives they have shared, or else can often be found at their local beach with their fur children - two cheeky dogs!

www.ingramcontent.com/pod-product-compliance
Lightning Source LLC
Chambersburg PA
CBHW050242220526
45465CB00002B/512